KATIE

A silly little thing
from me.

Love

D1152399

Purple Ronnie's
Little Guide to
DOING IT

♡

by Purple Ronnie

First published 1999 by Boxtree
an imprint of PanMacmillan Publishers Ltd.
20 New Wharf Road
London N1 9RR

www.macmillan.com

Associated companies throughout the world

ISBN 0 7522 7262 4

9 8 7

A CIP catalogue record for this book is
available from the British Library

Text by Giles Andreae
Illustrations by Janet Cronin
Printed and Bound in Hong Kong

a poem about
↓
Foreplay

Some men like to nibble

And some men like to stroke

But others simply drop
their pants

And shout "let's have
a poke!"

Things You Will Need

There are only 2 things you need for Doing It

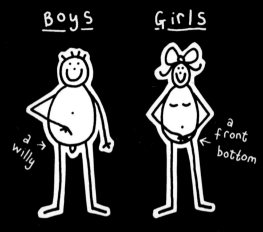

Getting in the Mood

Music is a great way of getting people in the mood for Doing It...

... make sure you get the right sort.

<u>Being Bare</u>

Most people like to be
bare when they are
Doing It

It is best not to laugh when they take their clothes off

a poem about

Willies

When girls say that size
doesn't matter

You know they don't mean
it at all

It's just a polite way of
saying

That yours is incredibly
small

Be Nice

Good lovers always make sure that the other person is having a nice time too

Special Tip

Doing It on the floor can be fun, but try not to get carpet burns on your bottom

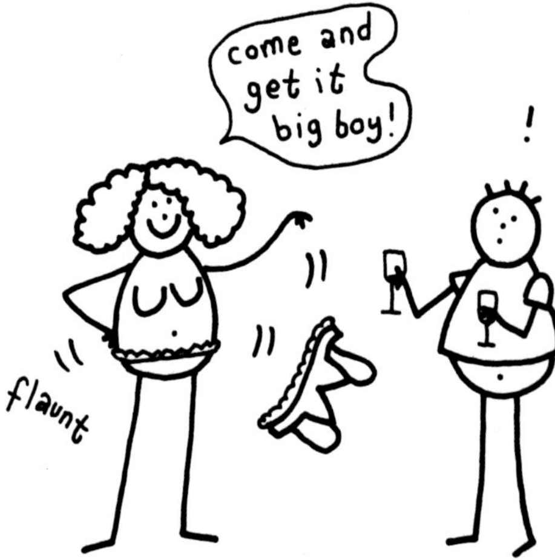
come and get it big boy!
!
flaunt

a poem about
Girls

Some girls hide under the
duvet
Then peel off their clothes
bit by bit
But others love flaunting
their gorgeous basoomers
And instantly dropping
their kit

Shouting Names

Some people get turned on if you shout out their name while you're Doing It...

... make sure you know
what they are called first.

Special Tip

There are lots of things you can find in the Kitchen that make Doing It even more exciting

Outdoors

Doing It in public places can be fun but try to make sure they're not <u>too</u> public

a poem about
↓

Fantasies

Some girls dream they'll
fall in love
With aliens from Mars
But others just want
rampant sex
With oily men in
cars

<u>Safety</u>

When Doing It with
someone for the first
time it is always
best to use protection

Surprises

Some people make
Doing It more exciting
by taking their lover
by surprise

Things not to say while Doing It

Men

1. How's your Mum?

2. What's on telly?

3. Come on!

<u>Girls</u>

1. Is it in yet?

2. zzzzzz

3. Have you finished?

a poem about
↓
Doing It

Some people just love to
Do It

In cars or in buses or
trains

But nothing compares

To that feeling you get

When you shag in the
lavvies of planes

The Shower

The best thing about
Doing It in the shower...

...is that nobody has to sleep in the wet patch

Special Trick

If you want to Do It
with someone really
sexy tell them it's
their minds you fancy

a poem about

↓

Sex

Girls say it feels like a
boiling hot river

Or waves crashing into
the shore

But boys say it's more like
a really good fart

Or watching your football
team score

Making It Last

Men sometimes need to think of something completely different to make it last

It is best not to tell girls
what you are thinking of

<u>After Doing It</u>

You should always cuddle, hug and kiss for at least 10 minutes after Doing It...

...that way girls will know that you like them too.

a poem about

Loving

It's all very well to be hung
                like a hippo

And make ladies squeal
                with delight

But sometimes they much
    prefer someone who cares

To be holding them
        closely all night